Radiance

Louis Nowra

Currency Press, Sydney

CURRENCY PLAYS

First published in 1993
by Currency Press Pty Ltd,
PO Box 2287, Strawberry Hills, NSW, 2012, Australia
enquiries@currency.com.au
www.currency.com.au
in association with Belvoir, Sydney
First published with *Radiance the screenplay* in 2000
Reprinted as a single edition 2014 in association with Belvoir, Sydney
Reprinted as a single edition 2015, 2019

Cataloguing-in-Publication data for this title is available from the National Library
of Australia.
Typeset by Dean Nottle for Currency Press.
Cover design by tomorrowpeople.

Currency Press acknowledges the Traditional Owners of the Country on which we
live and work. We pay our respects to all Aboriginal and Torres Strait Islander
Elders, past and present.

Contents

To Rosalba Clemente
and
Rachel Perkins

Radiance was first produced at the Belvoir Street Theatre, Sydney, on 21 September 1993 with the following cast:

MAE	Rachael Maza
CRESSY	Lydia Miller
NONA	Rhoda Roberts

Director, Rosalba Clemente
Set Design, Brian Thomson
Costume Design, Sue Field
Lighting Design, Fiona Johnstone
Sound Design, Paul Charlier
Stage Manager, Loretta Busby

CHARACTERS

MAE

CRESSY

NONA

SETTING

The play is set in North Queensland.

ACT ONE

SCENE ONE

The large living room of a wooden house on stilts. It is late morning and harsh tropical light pours in through the slats in the many shutters. MAE *is wearing a dowdy black frock and is lost in thought as she stares at a chair.* MAE *touches the chair with her foot as if making sure that there is no-one there. As she talks she strikes matches and throws them at the chair.*

MAE: Are you still there? You are, aren't you? I'll have to burn down this place to get rid of you. Ghosts burn, did you know that? And you'll burn. It'll all burn down, even ghosts can't live in a place that doesn't exist anymore. I'll do it. I'll have the courage. Everything will burn. And then you'll be gone. The whole world will burn. I'll hold my hands out, like warming them before a fire. [*She looks at a piece of paper in her hand and then at the chair. To the chair*] He did the dirty on you. Did the dirty on us both. He'll see it burning, but he'll be too late. They'll see it burning from miles and miles around. Like cracker night. Everything up in flames.

   NONA *enters wearing what can only be described as 'a little black dress'. She is also made up as if heading off to a party.* MAE, *surprised by* NONA*'s sudden appearance, hides the piece of paper from* NONA.

[*Shocked*] You can't wear that.
NONA: Why not?
MAE: Not to your mother's funeral.
NONA: I'm not fully dressed yet. I've still got to put on my knickers.
MAE: The dress. I meant the dress.
NONA: What's the matter with it?
MAE: You're almost naked.
NONA: If I was I wouldn't be wearing it. I can't get by without my little black dress. [*She goes to her open suitcase, its clothes are neatly stacked.*] You been at my suitcase?

MAE: Just tidying up.

NONA: [*scattering clothes*] It just makes things harder to find. You got any black knickers?

MAE: [*irritated*] We'll never get there!

> MAE *goes into the other room.* NONA *holds up an even shorter dress, this time red, against her body.*

NONA: [*calling out*] What about red? Or is that bad taste at your mum's funeral?

MAE: [*off*] Yes.

NONA: [*half to herself*] Is that yes, it's bad taste, or yes, wear the red? [*She throws the dress back on the suitcase and takes out some black high heels. Calling out*] I bought these shoes especially for today.

> NONA *turns on the radio then lifts up her dress and with a pair of tweezers starts to pluck her pubic hair. On the radio is* DOYLE, *the local priest.*

DOYLE: 'The world is full of temptation. As it should be. Because it is only by confronting temptation that we confront ourselves and become victorious over ourselves...'

MAE: [*off*] No black, what about white?

NONA: [*to herself, incredulous at* MAE*'s bad taste*] White!

DOYLE: 'The Lord will forgive sin but He will not forgive evil and many people have evil in their hearts. They may not do evil unto others, but they think evil and to think evil is as great as committing an evil deed. There are people in this town, yes, in this very town, who work, shop, play sports; seemingly good, generous people, but in their hearts is evil, evil that festers, evil that thinks evil of others and those people are just as severe sinners as those who commit evil deeds...'

> MAE *enters holding a black dress and stops stunned as she sees an unconcerned* NONA *pluck out her pubic hair.*

MAE: What are you doing?

NONA: Making the perfect bikini line.

MAE: Why don't you just shave the whole lot off and be done with it?

NONA: It would only attract child molesters.

> NONA*'s answer throws* MAE.

[*Referring to the radio*] Who's the nutter?

MAE: Father Doyle.

NONA: The one who's doing the service?

MAE *nods.*

I hope he doesn't go on like that at Mum's funeral. [*She turns the radio onto another station.*] Hey, do they still have listings of what's on? Like sports day? Who's in hospital? Rodeos? I was kind of hoping there was a rodeo in town. My father could be in town. Maybe he heard about Mum's death.

MAE: [*abruptly turning off the radio*] There's no rodeo in town. [*Holding out the dress*] I want you to put this on.

NONA: [*taking it with distaste*] This? [*Putting it against her body*] I look like a frump.

MAE: It's respectful. You have to respect the dead.

NONA: Why? It wouldn't be me. Mum wouldn't recognise me in this.

MAE: [*irritated with her*] Just try it on.

NONA: I'll dip it in mud and go grunge. I'll do up this place grunge. Anything would be better.

MAE: You don't like the way I've done it up?

NONA: I'm pretty good at decoration. Now that it's ours—

MAE: Things still have to be sorted out.

NONA: What things?

MAE *looks at the mess* NONA *has already created around her suitcase and gives an exasperated sigh.*

MAE: Your place must be like a pigsty.

NONA: [*starting to undress*] I'm a pig.

MAE *picks up the red dress and puts it against herself.*

MAE: My God, it's like wearing a handkerchief. You don't wear this in public.

NONA: [*putting the black dress over her dress*] Where else would I wear it?

NONA *gazes glumly at the dress. Indeed, it is frumpy looking.*

Do you wear this one?

MAE: It's not mine. It's Mum's.

NONA: I can't wear a dead woman's clothes.

MAE: She didn't die in it.

NONA: What did she die in?

MAE: You serious?

NONA: Oh, yes. When I die I want to look a beautiful corpse. The sort that turns every man into a necrophiliac. What was she wearing?

Pause. MAE *looks at* NONA *wondering if* NONA *is pulling her leg, but she seems serious.* NONA *sits in the chair to put on her high heels.*

MAE: I can't remember… just a nightgown, with a dressing-gown, I think.

NONA: Where did she die? Not where I slept last night? I'm not sleeping there tonight.

MAE: Here. That chair.

NONA *jumps up.*

NONA: Shit! You serious?

MAE: In that chair. Around this time. Late morning. I'd come back from shopping in town and there she was. Like she was sleeping. Purple lips. Dried saliva on her chin.

NONA: Did she look happy?

MAE: She looked empty. Hollow. Like if you tapped her, there would only be a hollow sound.

NONA: What were her last words?

MAE: I said I was shopping.

NONA: I mean the last words you heard.

MAE: Gurgle, gurgle…

NONA *pretends she hasn't heard* MAE*'s sarcastic reply and walks in her high heels, testing them out.*

NONA: I should have worn them in.

MAE: Don't wear them if they hurt.

NONA: No pain makes a girl plain. [*Indicating* MAE*'s dress*] You'll need the gumboots for your outfit. I hate this dress.

MAE: I want you to wear it for the funeral.

NONA: It's not me. I bet Cressy is going to wear something stylish. I bet you. And I'll look awful.

MAE: She's not coming.

NONA: What?

MAE: She said it was too far away.

NONA: Why didn't you tell me? You're always hiding things from me.

MAE: No, I'm not. I told you she was in London.

NONA: [*looking at a CD cover*] She looks great. You've never seen her on stage, have you?

MAE *shakes her head.*

I saw her in *Madame Butterfly*. In Adelaide. I didn't tell her I was coming. I dragged my boyfriend along. She was fantastic. You know, dying at the end, singing her heart out, killing her kid. So I ask to go backstage. I tell this creep on the door that she's my sister. Bouncers are such arseholes. And there she is. In her dressing-room. Like a florist shop. She's sitting in her chair, the mirror lights around her like some sort of halo. She's still got her make-up on—Jap eyes, white skin, like a mask. You know the only photo she had in her dressing-room? Me, when I was about five. Can you beat that? I tell her how much I liked *Madame Butterfly* and she goes '*Madama Butterfly*'. Like, how was I to know? It was my first opera. My boyfriend was a bit out of place—he only liked Acid Jazz—so he went out to wait for me and Cressy says, 'Oh, he's so handsome, Nona, but thick as a brick'.

MAE: That's terrible.

NONA: He was just a bloke, right? Dead ordinary. I stayed with him longer than I would have just to prove her wrong, but she was right.

NONA *laughs,* MAE *is bemused.*

MAE: Did you go out with her—

NONA: It was great. Japanese. I mean, like she was still in character, so we had to eat Japanese. On the floor. We had that horseradish stuff that burns your mouth. [*Pause.*] Why did you buy it, you don't have a CD player?

MAE: [*shrugging*] Seeing she doesn't send us any, I thought I may as well. Didn't even get a discount because she's my sister. [*Beat.*] Half price for a half sister.

NONA: It still makes her your sister. Two halves make a whole.

MAE: [*gazing at the CD cover*] She looks... different.

NONA: It's all make-up. I look really different when I'm photographed.

MAE: [*pointing to the red dress*] Is that how you like looking? Like a street walker?

NONA *is so astonished by* MAE*'s outburst, she almost laughs. Silence.*

NONA: [*pointing to the chair*] Was it always there?

MAE *is puzzled.*

Did she always sit there, in that spot?

MAE: Towards the end.

NONA: Because she wanted to watch the sea?

MAE: Who knows what was going on in her noggin?

NONA: I've never seen a dead person.

MAE: There's no art to dying. It's shitting, farting, crying, pissing yourself. That's how most people die, Nona.

NONA: You were born a nurse.

MAE: That's how people die.

NONA: I bet you she was looking at the island.

CRESSY *enters and stands there, smiling, expectant. She is dressed in a stylish and expensive black dress. Silence.* MAE *and* NONA *are surprised to see her.*

CRESSY: You can tell a small town, everyone leaves their front doors unlocked.

Silence.

NONA: [*pleased, praising her*] You look deadly.

CRESSY: Bit jet-lagged.

MAE: [*incredulous*] Cressy…

MAE *doesn't know how to react to her sister's appearance.*

CRESSY: [*smiling to* MAE] I'm no ghost.

An awkward pause. CRESSY *seems tense, uneasy to be back in the house.*

It's so hot.

NONA: I'll get you a glass of water.

CRESSY *puts her travelling valise on the chair.*

Don't!

CRESSY: Why?

NONA: Mum died there.

NONA *then rushes out. Puzzled,* CRESSY *picks up a burnt match, one of several on the chair.*

MAE: I was trying to set fire to it.

CRESSY: I came through town from the airport. Not much has changed. Like the dirt road here. The six palms along the beach have gone.

MAE: Rotted, so they were cut down.

CRESSY: Taxi drivers always keep their windows open. I've got dust in my throat. [*Beat.*] I'm heading back tomorrow.

MAE: Whatever you like.

CRESSY: I can stay in town.

NONA *enters and gives* CRESSY *a glass of water.*

MAE: The motel on Johnston Street's got new air conditioning.

MAE *exits.* CRESSY *looks to* NONA *as if she can give some reason for* MAE*'s abruptness.*

NONA: She's a bit tense. The funeral, I guess.

Pause.

CRESSY: I forgot how hot it gets in the tropics. I'm dripping.

NONA: Late this afternoon it'll be the sea breeze. Mae said you weren't coming.

CRESSY: I told her. [*Pause.*] We need the breeze, there's hardly any air.

NONA: I could get you a fan only it's broken.

CRESSY: [*not greatly liking the water*] Tap water. [*Looking around*] Not so down at heels, the house.

NONA: Mae did it up. Now it's ours we'll do it up properly.

CRESSY: Smaller. [*Opening her valise*] What time's the funeral?

NONA: Soon. I think. Well, Mae's been fussing around, so I think it's soon.

CRESSY *takes out a stylish black hat.*

Chic.

CRESSY: We'll kill 'em at the gravesite.

NONA *laughs.* CRESSY *stares at* NONA *making her a little uncomfortable.*

NONA: I've got pimples or something?

CRESSY: [*with a nervous laugh*] No… I forgot how grown-up you are, that's all.

MAE *enters with two hats.*

MAE: I've got some hats.
CRESSY: I brought mine with me.
MAE: For me and Nona.

She gives one to NONA.

NONA: I am not wearing this. It's ultra, ultra daggy, Mae.

MAE *hands her the other one.*

Mega daggy.
MAE: [*trying on one*] Suit yourself.
CRESSY: You've done the house up well. The shutters, the walls, everything.
MAE: Two years. I had time on my hands.
NONA: Who's going to be there?

MAE *shrugs.* NONA *notices* CRESSY *pacing.*

Sit down, Cressy.
CRESSY: Been cooped up in the aeroplane.
NONA: It's like you've taken some bad speed.

CRESSY *goes to sit down.*

MAE: [*to* CRESSY] No time to sit down, we have to make tracks.

NONA *closes the shutters, running rapidly from one to the other, talking as she does so.*

NONA: [*looking at* MAE] Do you really think you should wear that hat?
MAE: I like it.

NONA *suddenly takes off the dress, revealing her 'little black dress' underneath.*

NONA: I have to wear this; it's me.
MAE: You planning to pick up a mortuary assistant?

NONA *starts to plough through her suitcase and takes out a vermillion wig and a strawberry blonde one.*

NONA: Why should people look bad at a funeral? [*Holding up the wigs*] Which one?
CRESSY: [*bemused*] Whatever makes you feel good.
NONA: [*putting on the vermillion wig*] This one, then.

CRESSY *and* MAE *exchange glances.* CRESSY *looks* NONA *up and down.*

CRESSY: [*referring to* NONA*'s dress*] If brevity is the soul of wit then your dress will be worth a few laughs at the gravesite.

NONA: Better than waterworks.

MAE: Come on, we should be going. [*To* CRESSY] My car's a bit battered, is that okay?

NONA: You'd have to be a real idiot to steal that car.

MAE *heads out, the others follow after a pause.*

[*To* CRESSY] The car's old, but, of course, it hasn't got a scratch.

CRESSY *laughs. Pause.*

MAE: [*off, exasperated*] Nona!

NONA *tears in and runs to her suitcase to get another wig.*

NONA: I need my other wig.

SCENE TWO

The same place. Afternoon. CRESSY *enters, quietly angry.* NONA *follows carrying a small wooden box of ashes, then* MAE *enters.*

NONA: Why didn't anyone else come?

MAE: [*annoyed*] I don't know.

NONA: Didn't you send out any RSPCAs?

MAE: I said I don't know. Leave off me.

NONA: Great funeral. Didn't even get to bury her. Just a damn box with her ashes. I couldn't have done it better.

MAE: You should talk.

NONA: What do you mean?

MAE: Father Doyle. The service. Nothing on underneath.

NONA: You didn't have any black panties.

MAE: He was staring right up your dress. You must have known.

NONA: I was thinking about Mum.

MAE: Our mum's funeral. You showing off your twat, the priest with a hard-on.

NONA: And no-one except us turning up.

CRESSY: It's like a furnace in here.

> NONA *opens the shutters.* CRESSY *takes a bottle of champagne out of the bag she brought with her.*

Let's have this.

MAE: Water will be fine.

NONA: Mae... champagne! Just a drop. It's a wake. We have to have a wake! Loosen up. Where's the glasses?

> NONA *exits. Silence.* CRESSY *presses the cold champagne bottle against her cheek.*

CRESSY: You looked surprised when I turned up.

MAE: Didn't expect you.

CRESSY: But I phoned from London.

MAE: Yes... but I still didn't expect you to come back here.

CRESSY: Why?

MAE: Don't know... just didn't expect you to come back.

> NONA *enters with three different sorts of glasses.*

NONA: Why don't we send out for some pizzas?

MAE: I've made something.

> MAE *exits.*

NONA: I'll order a double pizza for you. All opera singers are fat, so you should put on more weight. [*Noticing a picture of Jesus with exposed heart*] Mae's picture of Jesus with the exposed heart. Gory, eh? She must have put the wrong date in the newspaper. She's going weird. [*Pause.*] Mum said our relatives were scattered across the whole country, probably haven't heard yet. At least Harry Wells sent a wreath.

CRESSY: It was from the Wells' family.

NONA: [*referring to the box of ashes*] What are we going to do with her?

CRESSY: Scatter them, I guess.

NONA: Where?

CRESSY: In the garden. Under the frangipani. She liked frangipani.

NONA: Did she?

> MAE *enters with some savories.*

MAE: I've only got these.

> CRESSY *starts to open the champagne bottle.*

CRESSY: I haven't had Bollinger since I was singing *La Traviata* in Milan.

MAE: What's that? A suburb in Brisbane?

NONA: Where are we going to put Mum?

The champagne cork goes up with a loud bang.

[*Crying out with delight*] Champagne!

MAE *holds out glasses and* CRESSY *pours the champagne.* NONA *puts the box on the chair and starts to wolf down the biscuits.*

She should stay in her chair. It's eerie to think that's her, isn't it? How do we know it is?

CRESSY: What?

NONA: [*taking a glass*] I heard this story about a man who had his parrot cremated and when he checked the ashes found dog bones in it. It was a big scandal in America.

CRESSY: [*sardonically*] We'll check it for dog bones.

NONA: [*seriously*] Oh, God, you do it.

CRESSY: A toast.

NONA: What to?

Pause.

CRESSY: Mum, I suppose.

MAE: You don't toast the dead.

NONA: No, you incinerate them.

CRESSY: To… to us.

The three clink glasses.

TRIO: To us.

NONA: [*to* MAE] You like it?

MAE: Don't know me French from me Australian.

NONA: [*gobbling more biscuits*] This is like last time.

CRESSY: Last time?

NONA: The three of us. [*To* MAE] You were on holiday break from the nursing school. [*To* CRESSY] You were passing through from the convent to Sydney. I was five. We had a picnic—underneath the six palms. Mum. Us. [*To* CRESSY] You took pictures of me. [*Pause.*] Lots.

CRESSY: [*smiling*] Yes.

NONA: We drank lemonade. Different now, eh? [*Beat.*] You know what it was?

MAE, *bemused, shakes her head.*

It was good. [*Pause.*] It was good.

CRESSY *stands at the open windows, face to the breeze.*

CRESSY: That feels nice. Where's that ferry going?

MAE: Coming back from Nora Island. The Japs have built a resort there.

NONA: I had a Japanese lover.

They look at her.

Just to see what it was like. If it was true.

CRESSY: True?

NONA: If they've got small dicks or not. [*Beat.*] It's true.

Pause.

MAE: Is that all you do?

NONA: What do you mean?

MAE: Have affairs with men?

NONA: Well, I'm not into women.

CRESSY: What exactly do you do?

NONA: What do you mean?

CRESSY: For a living.

NONA: You two think I'm a whore or something?

CRESSY: What about that boy you were with when you came backstage?

NONA: He wasn't a pimp or anything: he was a real estate salesman. He wanted to shift to Adelaide, so I came with him. You didn't like him.

CRESSY: No. That's why I didn't go out to dinner with you—I thought he'd tag along.

She continues, not noticing NONA'*s embarrassment.*

What exactly do you do?

NONA: For a job? [*Shrugging*] Bit of this, bit of that. I get by.

CRESSY: And where do you live?

NONA: Here, for a while.

MAE: She came yesterday, unannounced, of course, with all her goods and chattels.

NONA: It wasn't that much.

MAE: It's everywhere. Scattered everywhere. [*To* CRESSY] There's a chemical laboratory in the bathroom.

NONA: [*irritated*] I'll clean the bathroom.

CRESSY: You brought everything?

MAE: The guy she was living with kicked her out.

NONA: He was nice.

CRESSY: But he kicked you out.

NONA: Because I trashed his car.

CRESSY: So what are you going to do?

NONA: Mae said I could say here as long as I liked.

MAE: I said no such thing.

NONA: Christ, I'll only stay for a short time then. Anyway, I hate this town. Small towns! Hate them. I was so pleased the day I left. I'd just come back up the beach and the radio was on, and this announcer was saying that there was a rodeo on in Rocky. The biggest for ten years. Mum was asleep on the couch. I wrote her a note and said I was off to Cairns—but I was really off to Ayr, just in case she thought of following me. I was bored living here in this place. Just me and Mum. You two were gone. I knew she'd understand. Pretty neat for a fifteen-year-old, eh?

CRESSY: But why Ayr?

NONA: The rodeo! If it was the biggest in ten years then Dad was sure to be there.

CRESSY: Your father?

NONA: You never met him?

CRESSY: Why should I have met him?

NONA: Mum said he was really handsome. People called him the Black Prince. Every night I went to sleep dreaming of him. I know he was a bit of a bastard for leaving Mum, but, you know, he was my dad. I'd never seen him, not even a picture, but I knew I'd recognise him. He'd be tall, handsome. The Black Prince. 'Course, he wasn't there in Ayr. But when I saw the bucking horses, men trying to ride them, the bullocks, and the smells and crowd, I sensed him, sensed this would be the type of place he'd be. I took up with this bloke. Went with him from rodeo to rodeo thinking I would come across Dad. That one day there would be this man, this guy, standing tall in his cowboy boots, leaning against a verandah post. You know, the silent type. He'd be grinning and I'd see him in me. Our eyes: they'd be the same and he'd recognise me, recognise that he had created me. Then I found out that the bloke I was with was married with four kids so I came back here. And in I come, I walk in and there's Mum in bed with this guy. And she smiles and hugs me like I'd never really been away all those months, so I thought, she's okay by herself—time I pissed off again, I knew I could look after myself. [*Beat.*] Maybe, now, the Black Prince'll hear about Mum dying and track me down, eh? [*Beat.*] And we'll all get to meet him.

> CRESSY *doesn't answer, instead she pours each one some more champagne.*

MAE: No.

> *She covers the glass with her hand.*

CRESSY: I'll pour it on your hand and it'll stain the floor.
NONA: It's French, Mae!
CRESSY: Mae!

> CRESSY *pours* MAE *some champagne.*

MAE: I don't drink much.
CRESSY: What an awful box.
NONA: Let's put her in something better.

> *She exits quickly.*

MAE: Where you going?

> *An awkward silence.*

CRESSY: Did she die in pain?

> MAE *shakes her head.*

MAE: She's only been here twenty-four hours and eaten me out of house and home.

> *Pause.*

CRESSY: I never knew she went off on the rodeo circuit.
MAE: [*bemused*] Will o' the wisp.
CRESSY: [*bitterly*] The Black Prince… [*Pause.*] Sorry about the money: the funeral. I didn't think.
MAE: That's okay. I wasn't expecting you to.
CRESSY: [*irritated*] I've sent money to help you.
MAE: It helped fix up the house.
CRESSY: It was for you, not her.

MAE: You should have seen it when I arrived—unbelievable. A rundown shack. Like it might blow away if you breathed on it. The day I arrived some couple walked through the house taking pictures. They thought it was derelict. I threw them out. [*With a rueful smile*] Yelling at them: 'It's my home! Get out. It's my home!' I think it was the home, more than Mum, that made me stay. [*Motioning to the house*] So, it's due to you. Thank you.

CRESSY: You don't have to thank me.

NONA *enters with a glass vase.*

NONA: What about this? We can see them then.

MAE: [*angrily*] No.

NONA: She didn't have a proper funeral. You messed up the funeral. We should do something proper.

MAE: Stick to what you know best—men.

NONA: What's this thing about men?

MAE: I don't know how you can behave the way you do.

NONA: Because I like it. I like being with a man. I like sex. I like the feel and smell of a man.

MAE: You look cheap.

NONA: My clothes are always expensive. Anyway, what would you know, you don't know me?

MAE: At least I don't live off men.

NONA: What the fuck do you mean?

MAE: Don't swear.

NONA: I have never lived off a man. I have never taken money from a man for sex.

CRESSY: Nona...

NONA: No, she's been picking on the way I dress since I arrived. Looking at me like I'm a slut or something. [*To* MAE] I have never taken a penny. Like Mum. That's what you hate about me. I like men. Like Mum liked them. She never took a penny.

MAE: Look how she ended up. Deserted by them.

NONA: She had memories. She had a good time. Harry Wells loved her. He gave her this house.

MAE: He was a bastard! But then Mum always picked them. She had no morals. That's like you. No willpower. I did this house, I looked after her. I gave up a private life. Just for her.

NONA: Because you love playing the martyr.

MAE: If you loved her so much, why didn't you come up here and look after her? Why didn't you clean up the shit?

NONA: Because you said you wanted to look after her. Besides, I have no morals, do I?

MAE: You don't get it, do you? She hurt so many people—

NONA: She didn't hurt me.

MAE: Because you were the one she kept.

NONA: Kindred spirits, eh?

MAE: I cringed in my bed when I'd hear that knocking on the flywire screen door. Then I'd hear her footsteps down the hallway, smell her cheap perfume, and her voice—not Mum's voice, this tiny girl's voice, like a fourteen-year-old on her first date. [*Parodying it*] 'Hi, Mister Gorgeous'—and these male voices—and this laughing—not real laughter, fake laughter because all they wanted to do was to get her into bed.

NONA: [*to* CRESSY, *remembering with pleasure*] I'd rush in to her bedroom the next morning, after I'd hear her new man go, I'd throw myself onto the bed and she'd be there, happy, contented, you know, and I'd press my face into the sheets and pillows and smell her new man and I'd be high on this new smell, excited, high, like Mum. And she'd talk about him, like this new one was the real one, the real Prince and we'd giggle and laugh.

MAE: [*to* CRESSY] How could she see it that way?

NONA: Don't know. I just did.

MAE: Didn't you ever feel you wanted a father—

NONA: He'd gone.

MAE: No, I mean, one who would be a father to you?

NONA: [*irritated*] Christ, I don't know. Mum used to say that men and women can't live together. I mean, just before coming up here, I give the flick to this guy. He chases me. Pleads with me. So I stay in some motel with him for a couple of days, going balmy, just staring at the vomit-green curtains and watching all the soaps. He with one eye always open, watching me, guarding me. One night he's finally asleep, so I nick off. He chases after me. Gets me in the next town. Drags me around the back of the bus shelter. He punches me almost out cold. Then he starts crying saying, 'Why do you make me hit you?' And I think, 'Hey, I'm the one with the black eye. I'm the one who's hurt!'

Silence.

MAE: You'll end up like her.

NONA: [*defiantly*] Good. [*Pause.*] Hey, we're all unattached. We could live together here. Get old together.

MAE *laughs out loud, startling the other two.*

What's so funny?

MAE: I have no idea what planet you come from. Maybe your father was an alien.

NONA: [*amused*] The Black Prince has gone back to his own planet. The dark side of the moon.

MAE: That's where they've all gone. [*Pointing to* CRESSY] Your father. Mine's in heaven, I think. [*To* NONA] And yours is in hell, the very pit of hell.

NONA *laughs, thinking* MAE *is joking.* MAE *laughs, noticing the empty plate.*

Oh, God, I need some food in my stomach—I'll get some more. [*Aside to* NONA *as she exits*] Gutsface…

CRESSY: [*looking out at the sky*] The sky's greening. Full of electricity. [*Pause.*] You look happy.

NONA: Oh, the champagne. Being home. I've been thinking about this place a lot. [*Beat.*] Have to. Kinda broke. Stone broke. We could go thirds in the house. I haven't talked to Mae about it, but we should, shouldn't we?

CRESSY: If we sold the house what would you do with the money?

NONA: Oh, I know you and Mae think I'm a bit of a flake, but I have plans. I'm going to open a wig shop. It's the new trend. I've decided that's what I'm going to do. I'm a late starter. I'm ambitious, you know.

CRESSY: It's got to be more than that. You've got to sacrifice. Go without things. Can you do that? A lot of the producers and musicians think I am a bitch. But everything has to be right. If they get the music wrong, I sound bad, if they get the set wrong, I look stupid. I've sacrificed everything, to do what I want to do. You have to do that.

NONA: I'm going to, I'm going to. [*Looking out the windows*] Didn't you do that?

CRESSY: Do what?

NONA: Go down to the beach to collect mussels. And the mud crabs. You go into restaurants now and they're a fortune. It was poor man's food then.

CRESSY: I can't eat it when I'm at a restaurant. Reminds me of catching them. [*Illustrating*] Claws waving like this and then—

NONA: [*demonstrating*] Pounce!

CRESSY: String—

NONA: Fucking big stick if needed.

> *They laugh.*

And turtle. We should get a turtle; have it tonight.

> CRESSY *laughs.*

You'd love it. [*Suddenly on another track*] We'll walk across to the island tonight. Take some champagne and food. Dig for turtles, eat them on the island. Mum always wanted to do that. It'll be great, Mae said low tide's later on tonight. Walk across the mudflats to the island. Get the Japs to buy us cocktails. Great, eh? We'll have to keep an eye on Mae, though: she's a world famous criminal and will be nicking the ashtrays and stuff.

CRESSY: [*bemused*] I can never tell whether you're serious or not.

NONA: [*pleased*] Home is where the heart is. You like it?

CRESSY: [*shrugging*] I never really liked it.

NONA: You prefer posh hotels, right?

CRESSY: It's not that. [*Beat.*] It makes my stomach knot. [*Beat.*] I just need to breathe. I forgot about living up here—just before it breaks, a storm sucks up all the air. Breathless.

NONA: Mum always loved this place. It was the only thing she had. She said Harry Wells gave it to her as a present. Important man up here. The biggest sugar plantation.

CRESSY: He was scared that his wife would find out about him and Mum, so he gave her this holiday shack to keep her quiet.

NONA: Mum would never have said anything.

CRESSY: Men never trust a woman. You should know that, Nono.

NONA: [*laughing*] I haven't been called that for years. Nono, always says 'yes yes'.

They both laugh.

Harry should have come. We wouldn't have said anything. But men are real cowards like that. At least he left Mum the house. It was a sign of his love. See, Mum was loved. [*Quietly, referring to* MAE] She thinks I'm a slut.

CRESSY: But you are.

NONA *is stunned by* CRESSY'*s comment.*

It's just a word, Nona.

Pause.

NONA: You are embarrassed by me, aren't you? That night I came backstage. You were embarrassed.

CRESSY: Just surprised to see you.

NONA: Embarrassed. Treating me like a stranger. Yet you had my picture on the dressing table.

CRESSY: I like it, you looked cute.

NONA: You sat there, like you didn't know how to talk to me.

A beat.

CRESSY: Don't be silly.

NONA: It was in the program—no mention of Queensland. Here. Mum. Mae. Me.

CRESSY: Nona, you don't put those kind of things in programs.

NONA: You're lying now like you lied in the program. That's okay, I lie all the time.

CRESSY: I'm not lying—

NONA: You wouldn't even go out to dinner with me. Ashamed, you were.

CRESSY: I could never, never be ashamed of you.

Pause.

NONA: All our fathers were aliens. [*Starting to spin, faster and faster. Calling out*] Mae—don't get any food, we're going turtle hunting! The world is spinning. You should take drugs. Is that what you get from singing? Do you get high?

CRESSY: Sometimes. When I'm singing, I think: Who's this singing? Whose voice has possessed me? [*Motioning to her throat*] Feel. Go on, feel it…

NONA *gingerly feels* CRESSY*'s throat.*

No, harder.

NONA: It's like gristle.

CRESSY: Harder—like you're strangling me.

NONA: No.

CRESSY: Go on. Harder. Squeeze it.

NONA: [*squeezing* CRESSY*'s throat*] It's like concrete. Gives me the heebie jeebies—

NONA *lets go.* CRESSY *smiles.*

CRESSY: Sacrifice.

NONA: Jeez, you'd be able to give great head.

CRESSY: You see those younger singers, full of themselves, and you feel their throats and it's like squeezing marshmallow.

NONA: Will you be doing an opera when you go back to London?

CRESSY: I'm having a bit of a rest from singing. A sabbatical.

NONA: You don't sing on Sundays, eh?

CRESSY *doesn't know if* NONA*'s joking or not.*

After a man had been, Mum and me would get up and have brekkie. She'd be really happy and she'd dance through here—making sure she didn't trip over the trussed-up turtles, of course, and she'd be singing—like you.

MAE: [*off*] Come and get it!

NONA: I said we're going to the island.

MAE: [*off*] Hey, guess what, I've found a bottle of wine under the sink.

NONA: [*quietly to* CRESSY] Found a bottle under the sink! It's like a wine cellar under there.

Both laugh. NONA *spots a movement outside, she hurries to the shutter.*

[*Excitedly*] He's here! He's here!

CRESSY: What?

NONA: The Black Prince.

MAE: [*entering with a bottle*] I'd forgotten all about it.

NONA: He's in the garden.

MAE: What?

NONA: [*excited, running from shutter to shutter*] Someone in the garden. It's the Black Prince.

CRESSY: Nona, don't be such a bloody idiot.

NONA: I bet you it is. I bet you he's come.

She starts to run outside.

MAE: [*stopping her*] It's not him.

NONA: It is! I told you. I told you both!

MAE: Nona!

Suddenly a huge hail of stones lands on the tin roof. CRESSY *and* NONA *look up, astonished by the racket, but* MAE *doesn't. She's heard this sound before and is scared, but tries not to let the others see.*

CRESSY: What is it?

NONA: Hailstones!

Boys' voices are heard chanting.

VOICES: Come out, you old witch!
　　　　Come out and play,
　　　　You stupid old bitch,
　　　　Come out, you old witch,
　　　　Come out, you old witch,
　　　　Come out and play!

Laughter.

CRESSY: [*to* MAE] What's happening?

MAE: It's just some boys.

Suddenly another hail of stones on the roof.

CRESSY: [*over the noise*] What are they doing?

MAE: Don't cause a fuss.

NONA: Stones. They're throwing stones at the house.

MAE: Only on the roof.

CRESSY: [*about to go outside*] I'm going to stop them.

MAE: [*grabbing her*] Don't.

It is quiet now.

You'll only egg them on.

VOICES: Come out, you stupid old bitch,
        Come out, you old witch.
        Witch! Witch! Witch!

More stones, only this time briefly. Then the laughter of the boys.
They continue to sing.

CRESSY: Do they do this a lot?
MAE: They're only boys.
CRESSY: [*irritated*] Mae! How often do they do this?
MAE: [*snapping*] I don't know!
NONA: Well, they're not fucking well going to do it again.

    NONA *runs outside.*

MAE: Nona!
CRESSY: What's happening, Mae? Why are they doing it?

    Beat.

MAE: I guess they don't know.
CRESSY: Know what?
MAE: That she's dead.
CRESSY: It's against Mum? Are they calling her a witch?
MAE: [*coldly smiling*] But she was. She was a witch.

    CRESSY *laughs at the outrageousness of it.*

She was.
NONA: [*off, yelling at the boys*] Get the fuck out of this garden! Go on,
    fuck off! I'll bloody smash your ugly faces in! Bastards! Piss off...

    MAE *does not hear* NONA *as the truth about the funeral service*
    pours out with great intensity.

MAE: She spat at people if I took her out. Cursed them. She turned into
a witch. A monster. She cursed everyone in the street, women, men,
children. Spat on them. Why do you think no-one turned up today?
No-one goes to a funeral service for a witch! That's why no-one
turned up—no-one goes to a funeral for a witch. [*Beat.*] I hate that
chair! That's where the witch sat all day long. I despise it. I'm going
to smash it up and burn it.

SCENE THREE

Same place. Hours later. It's evening. CRESSY *is looking through* NONA *'s untidy suitcase. Country and Western music ('The Wayward Wind') is playing on the radio and* CRESSY *hums along to it. She picks out the red wig and tries it on. From the kitchen we hear* MAE *and* NONA.

NONA: [*off*] Don't do them! Leave them in the sink!

MAE: [*off*] I want to. [*Laughing*] It soothes me.

NONA: [*off, laughing*] Soothes you?

> CRESSY *looks at her reflection in a small mirror she found in the suitcase and laughs.* NONA, *wearing a new dress and carrying a bag of stones, enters and watches* CRESSY.

What are you going to sing?

> CRESSY *reacts as if caught red-handed.*

[*Referring to the wig*] It looks good on you. Wear one of my dresses. I've changed. Go on.

CRESSY: Oh, God, no.

> NONA *drops the bag on the table.*

What's that?

NONA: A bag of stones, just in case those brats come back. [*She turns off the radio.*] That's what you should do—sing. For us.

> MAE *enters.*

Yes, yes, yes. Sing something for us.

MAE: Yes. I haven't heard you. Ever.

> CRESSY *laughs.*

NONA: Sing *Madame Butterfly*. You sang it beautifully. Do it.

CRESSY: [*irritated*] Do what?

NONA: Sing *Madama Butterfly*.

CRESSY: My voice is tired.

NONA: Act it out.

CRESSY: You're crazy.

NONA: I'll do it. I remember you doing it. [*She rushes to a suitcase and, throwing things out in gay abandon, searches for something.*] I bought it when I was living with my Japanese lover. Had to buy it myself. Japanese are stingy buggers. [*She pulls out a red kimono.*] Beautiful, eh? [*She whips off the vermillion wig and throws on a black wig.*] I remember it all. Total recall. It was in Italian.

She starts singing it and acting it out, but the words are nonsense words. NONA*'s performance is a parody of the aria 'Un Bel di Vedremo' ('One Fine Day') but there is something moving about it.* MAE *laughs but* CRESSY *is entranced by it.*

[*To* MAE] And then right at the end of the opera, she blindfolds her child, and grabbing a knife…

MAE: [*to* NONA] You shouldn't make fun of her.

NONA *stops.*

CRESSY: No, it's alright. You were good.

NONA: [*laughing*] Good?

CRESSY: [*seriously, almost enviously*] Yes. Your acting… it's sort of free…

NONA *laughs at the compliment.*

MAE: And she kills the child?

CRESSY: [*staring at* NONA] Herself. [*Professionally*] The wig—it doesn't suit you.

NONA: [*to the box of ashes*] You gave her your voice. [*To* MAE] She had a good voice, didn't she?

MAE *nods.*

MAE: She used to sing 'Goodnight, Irene'.

NONA: Never heard her sing that. Hey, let's go, it'll take us a few hours to get to the island.

MAE: You two go.

NONA: No, the three of us. It'll make up for the funeral. We'll make it up to her.

MAE: She's just ashes.

NONA: We have to—we're all she had. This is the only time during the year—only for two days can you walk over to it. Come on.

CRESSY: No. A storm's coming up… behind the island. The sky looks all bruised.

NONA: In the rain. The lightning!

CRESSY: You are crazy.

NONA: I love getting wet. Makes me brand new.

CRESSY: Maybe after it's passed.

MAE: You two go!

NONA: No, us three!

MAE: Listen to me! I don't want to. You two should go. Get out of the house. Leave me here.

The sound of thunder. The sisters listen.

CRESSY: Thunder.

NONA: Moving furniture in heaven.

CRESSY *goes to the window and stares outside at the gathering storm.*

CRESSY: The sky's full of electricity.

The other two look out.

NONA: The bats know. Look at them flying home.

She laughs. CRESSY *kisses her as if thanking her for the performance, but* NONA *is puzzled why her sister is kissing her.*

MAE: It's one of those storms that will pass over us.

A bolt of lightning, surprising the girls.

NONA: But we can still go to the island, can't we?

MAE: It's raining.

NONA: It'll pass. You know that. An hour or two. It's full moon tonight—then we'll walk across the flats under the full moon. [*Taking a pair of Doc Martens out of her suitcase*] You can wear these.

MAE: You wear these?

NONA: They're in, Mae.

MAE: You don't really wear them?

NONA: I'm a fashion victim. Look, it's not as if I'm going to a wedding or anything.

MAE: You probably would wear them to a wedding, wouldn't you?

NONA: Crikey, I'm not going to get married.

MAE: You're not like Mum. She always wanted to get married.

NONA: She didn't.

MAE: Ah, there's some things you don't know about her, Nono. Lots of things. You thought you knew her better than us.

MAE *exits.*

NONA: What she doing?

CRESSY *shrugs.*

CRESSY: [*looking out, breathing deeply*] The air is coming with the rain. [*Shouting*] Cool, cool air! I can breathe.

Pause.

NONA: Staying in air-conditioned hotel rooms, you mustn't be used to real air.

CRESSY *smiles.*

It must be great staying in those places, though.

CRESSY: The windows in most don't open. It's like being cut off from the world. Here I can reach out and touch things.

NONA: You have lots of lovers?

CRESSY: Men and me don't get on.

NONA: You spend your time in those posh hotels alone? What a waste.

CRESSY: I had a man who used to stay. Sort of.

NONA: Sort of?

CRESSY: I thought he stayed. There were no signs he was there… but I knew he stayed… I was on this disastrous tour of Europe… I took on a role when my voice wasn't ready for it. Every night I'd go out and try to sing it, but the music kept on overwhelming me. I felt like I was drowning. Every night I drowned. One morning I woke up and saw that all the furniture—writing tables, drawers, chairs, were all piled up on top of each other. I thought it was a practical joke by the musicians—a musician's idea of humour is a car accident— but the next morning, in a new city, there it was—all the furniture piled up again. Then the next town. I never heard a thing. I'd wake up in the morning, and there it'd be—these towers of furniture. I began to wake up in a sweat, wondering who was coming into my room at night and doing this while I slept. I blamed everyone, the musicians, the hotel staff, but it kept on happening. Maybe it was a poltergeist—

NONA: Oh, fuck, not a ghost story—I hate ghosts stories—they make me want to wee.

CRESSY: But it wasn't. Maybe it was a poltergeist. It began to affect my singing. Because while I was singing, I was thinking of what was going to happen that night when I slept. At the last moment, I'd change rooms and lie awake waiting for it to come in. Eventually I'd fall asleep and when I woke up—there it would be... my furniture piled up in the middle of the room. I didn't know what to do. I had someone sit with me all through the night. That helped, because it didn't come. Then one night I slept by myself and I woke up in the morning, not in my bed, but in the corner of the room. It had come in, lifted me out of my bed and put all the furniture on the bed. I was petrified. I didn't know what to do. I thought I heard it in the bathroom and so I cowered in the corner, huddled up in my blanket for hours, until my manager came and got me. I was late for my performance. The first time ever. I got her to check the bathroom but there was no-one there.

NONA: Did the poltergeist come back?

CRESSY: There was no poltergeist. I had done it... in my sleep. Overwork and strain, I guess.

NONA: It just goes to show that work's a curse. Mum always said that.

CRESSY: [*motioning to the box of ashes*] That stranger. That selfish woman. Look at us, we're strangers because of her. We have hardly been together. She had us without any concern for our future. No concern for me and Mae.

NONA: She was kind to me. When officials came, she always hid me.

CRESSY: You were special. When they came for Mae, she just handed her over. Easy as pie; like she did with me. And then forgot us.

NONA: She didn't. She was always talking about you two.

CRESSY: She knew where I was. Where Mae was. All she had to do was visit. Once.

NONA: She tried to.

CRESSY: Tried? All she had to do was ask the nuns.

NONA: She saw you. I was there. When I was very little. We took a train to Brisbane. And then we walked to the convent. She held my hand. I can still feel her hand, it was really damp. Trembling like a leaf. We walked halfway up the driveway and she turned back.

CRESSY: [*sarcastically*] Don't tell me the wind came up?

NONA: We stood behind some bushes outside the fence. Stood for what seemed like hours until lunchtime and there you were. Just for a second. You were walking between two nuns. I yelled out your name. Mum put her hand over my mouth and said, 'That's it, I just wanted to see her once. She's in safe hands', and we turned and walked back to the station.

CRESSY: Not good enough, Nono. Not good enough. Not to have a father and your mother not wanting to see you—

NONA: She wanted to—

CRESSY: Didn't want enough. On visiting days, some parents would come, even from interstate and there I'd be, me and a few other girls with no visitors. And because we had no visitors the nuns would get us to do the laundry. To pass the time. To pass the time! There we were, us girls in the steam and stink of the laundry, with its smell of starch and dirty clothes. At first I would make believe we were in hell and I'd curse the nuns, say that I'd fuck the devil, but one day I saw a picture in one of the nun's magazines. It was a film star playing a Polynesian princess, wearing a sarong, hibiscus in her hair. She looked so beautiful, so exotic, so far from the laundry. And so I pretended to be her. I'd wrap a tablecloth around me, put an hibiscus in my hair and sing to the other girls. They'd applaud me and I'd do it again and again, until I thought I was that princess, pretending the copper steam was the steam of a volcano I was about to throw myself into and sacrifice myself to the gods. But instead of throwing myself in, I won a singing scholarship. I came back here on the way to Sydney. Mum said the wind was coming up from the island. The ancestors were telling me not to go. I walked out that door and made it as a singer.

NONA: She'd had learnt by the time I came along. She didn't know what to do when they took you two.

CRESSY: She didn't fight for me.

NONA: What could she do? She had no husband. The law was against her. Living alone here with a kid, how could she defend herself? She was young. Forgive her. What could she have done? What do you want me to do? Get down on my knees and apologise for the fact that I stayed with her? [*Bitterly*] Mum and I were sluts, what more could you expect? Sluts don't write, we fuck!

CRESSY: [*slapping* NONA *across the face*] Shut up!

   There is a stunned silence.

NONA: You believe she was, don't you?

CRESSY: Did I hurt you?

NONA: It's nothing. Nothing.

CRESSY: I didn't mean to hurt you.

NONA: [*with mock happiness*] Oh, I've been roughed up by experts.

> MAE *enters, wearing a wedding dress, her hair flowing free.*

MAE: [*singing/dancing*]
> Step we gaily on we go,
> Heel to heel and toe to toe,
> Arm and arm and row and row,
> All for Marie's wedding.

> *She finishes her dance in front of* NONA.

[*Triumphantly*] It's hers.

CRESSY: It's not.

> NONA *is astonished at how* MAE *looks.*

NONA: You look like Mum.

> MAE *laughs at what she thinks is* NONA's *nonsense.*

The spitting image. [*To* CRESSY] With her hair out, doesn't she?

CRESSY: [*nodding*] A little…

MAE: I was cleaning up in her room, you know how messy she was, when I found it. She even lied it was hers—

NONA: She never married.

MAE: I found out from old Davis who runs the haberdashery that Mum had kept it on lay-by for two years, paying it off bit by bit.

NONA: To marry the Black Prince.

MAE: Harry Wells. He was the man she truly loved. He said he would leave his wife.

NONA: But that bitch wouldn't let him go.

MAE: He led her on, telling her he was getting a divorce and they would be married soon after. He gave her stuff—

NONA: This place?

MAE: No, not then. He kept on putting off the wedding, any excuse. This is where they met, their rendezvous. His wife found out and he returned to her.

NONA: I know blokes like that. In fact, they're all like that. Come on, let's go. Now, across the flats!

MAE: Why?

NONA: Because it won't happen for another year.

MAE: But why?

NONA: To scatter her ashes there. The three of us. [*Beat.*] We're all blood. Half of ourselves are her.

CRESSY: She might have wanted her ashes scattered somewhere else. Mae?

MAE: [*referring to* NONA] She never listens. I told her you two should do it.

NONA: I know she wanted her ashes scattered there. I know! [*Looking at the box*] Cressy is right; bloody pathetic things they stick the ashes in, isn't it? Come on, let's stick her in the vase. She liked vases.

MAE: You're going to put her in there?

NONA: Not me, too creepy. You or Cressy will do it.

CRESSY: Why do you want to put her in there?

NONA: Because it's so much better than the box. When we take her to the island, think how good she'll look.

MAE: We won't take her to the island.

NONA: [*stubbornly*] Yes.

MAE: We'll see.

NONA: We won't see. We'll do it. [*Pause. Referring to the ashes*] Please.

CRESSY: Mae, you were the nurse.

MAE: That'd be right, wouldn't it?

NONA: You must have done this all the time.

MAE: Nono, they were bodies, this is Mum's ashes.

NONA: So much the better. It's not a dead body, is it?

MAE: You're so keen to get her in there, you do it.

NONA: Alright.

> NONA *throws the vase at* CRESSY *who catches it and picks up the box of ashes. More thunder and lightning.*

MAE: Rain.

> *She closes some of the shutters.* NONA *opens the box, but appears paralysed on seeing the ashes.*

NONA: Just like someone's cleaned out the fireplace.

CRESSY: Nona… just tip them in here.

NONA: [*shaking her head*] I can't.

MAE: [*irritated*] Don't be silly. If you're going to do, do it.

She goes over to NONA *to take the box from her.*

NONA: No, don't, I can do it.

They both grab the box.

MAE: You'll be hours. Give it to me.

NONA: No, I can do it.

MAE: Give it to me.

They struggle. MAE *whips the box of ashes from* NONA *and in so doing sprays the ashes on herself and the others and the floor. The three women are wide-eyed in astonishment. Silence.*

NONA: You've spilt Mum on the floor.

CRESSY: [*wiping her dress*] On my dress, too.

NONA: Oh, my God, look what we've done to Mum.

She bursts into laughter.

MAE: Nona! [*Then she starts laughing. Pointing at* CRESSY] She ruined your dress.

The three are now laughing, almost hysterically.

NONA: She's everywhere.

MAE: We've scattered her.

CRESSY: What are we going to do? She's everywhere!

NONA: Mum, Mum, you're everywhere!

Their laughter dies down a little. Silence. They look at one another trying not to laugh.

CRESSY: I'm going to have to explain to the laundry, that's no stain, that's my mum.

They burst into laughter again and then stop.

NONA: We can't leave her on the floor. We have to clean her up.

The three try not laugh.

CRESSY: We can't pick her up, it's impossible...

NONA: I want to scatter her on the island. Not here.

CRESSY: We'll just have to pick her up.

NONA: We have to pick up every piece or else we'll be grinding her into the floor every time we walk in here. I'm probably standing on her nose. Ugh…

NONA: Come on, we'll put her in the vase.

MAE: No vase.

NONA: I've got it! The tin box. Radiance liquorice nougat.

CRESSY: What?

NONA: The tin box Mum had up on the fridge. She said that Italian fellow bought it for her. Even when it was empty it still smelt delicious.

MAE: You're not going to put Mum in a tin box.

NONA: It'll smell great.

She tears off into the kitchen. Pause. The two sisters look at one another. Wry smiles.

CRESSY: She doesn't need drugs.

They laugh. NONA *tears back in.*

NONA: I know where it is… under the house. With the trunk, where Mum kept our stuff.

MAE: You're not going to get it now?

CRESSY: Don't go under the house.

NONA: [*tearing back out*] I want the tin.

CRESSY: It's dark.

NONA: [*off*] Torch. Torch! Anyone want to join me under the house?

CRESSY: Get it in the morning.

NONA: [*entering with a torch*] I've got it. She's going to smell so terrific, we could eat her.

Off she goes, laughing.

CRESSY: It's going to be like having a willy-willy in the house having her stay. Did Mum leave this just to you?

MAE: What do you mean?

CRESSY: In the will.

MAE: There is no will. She didn't make one.

CRESSY: So you're taking it?

MAE: I'm going to burn it to the ground.

Pause.

CRESSY: What about Nona?

MAE: [*motioning to the suitcase*] Suitcases are her home.

CRESSY: But she might want this. She can have my share.

From under the house there is a 'spooky wailing' from NONA *and then a parody of maniacal laughter.*

Nona! Stop it. Get back here.

NONA: [*from under the house*] Here comes the midnight ghost! Here's the bogeyman!

More maniacal laughter.

CRESSY: [*agitated*] Nona! Get back here!

MAE: [*watching* CRESSY *closely*] What's the matter?

CRESSY: It's dark under there.

MAE: She's got a torch.

CRESSY: She's so stupid! [*To* NONA] Nona! Don't be such a bloody idiot! Do it in the morning!

MAE: Nona, get back up here!

CRESSY: [*almost angrily to* MAE] There's no need to do it for me! [*Quietly, attempting a smile*] Spiders are horrible things.

More thunder and lightning.

MAE: Smell the sky…

CRESSY: Burning air.

MAE: The lightning. [*Beat.*] Isn't it strange, how something you should be terrified of looks so enticing, so attractive? I've always been attracted to it. [*Picking up the bag of stones*] Nona'd throw them at those boys, wouldn't she? Wish I had the courage.

She throws a stone at the wall and laughs.

CRESSY: Careful.

A scream of delight from under the house.

NONA: [*off*] Found it!

MAE: I'm renovating. Fixing it up for Nona. Making her feel at home. [*She throws more stones at walls.*] The new look! [*Turning angrily, she some throws at the chair.*] Isn't that the worst chair in the world? [*Throwing more at the chair*] Let's pretend that's Harry Wells. And the boys—we mustn't forget the boys.

CRESSY *steps away and watches her sister laughing almost hysterically and throwing stones around the living room. One of the stones hits the box of ashes.*

Got you!

NONA *rushes in with the Radiance liquorice nougat tin.*

NONA: Found it! And guess what else? [*From behind her back she brings forth a battered black cowboy hat.*] His. I found it. The Black Prince's.

CRESSY: The Black Prince?

NONA: Yes, it is. Mum told me. She said he wore a cowboy hat.

CRESSY: [*angrily*] It's not his! [*She grabs the hat and throws it outside through the window.*] It's not his! It's a hat that belonged to one of her boyfriends.

NONA: It's his.

MAE: Nona! [*To* CRESSY] Tell her. [*Beat.*] Tell her.

CRESSY: [*coldly*] What?

NONA: Tell me what?

MAE: Cressy—tell her. [*Pause. Then angrily*] There was no rodeo star. No Black Prince.

CRESSY: What are you talking about?

MAE *looks to* CRESSY *to tell* NONA.

MAE: [*indicating* CRESSY] She was there.

NONA: There? You saw my father?

MAE: Tell her.

She throws a stone at CRESSY, *just missing her.*

Tell her! She should know.

CRESSY: There wasn't a Black Prince.

MAE: Tell her the truth. Mum's boyfriend… you were playing under the house.

CRESSY: Mum's boyfriend?

MAE: She was under the house. Under our feet. [*Pause.*] Do you want me to tell her?

CRESSY: No. [*Pause.*] No.

Pause.

MAE: [*going to tell the story*] Under the house—

CRESSY: [*not wanting* MAE *to tell the story*] Here—I heard a voice. A male voice. Here in the living room. He was in here. I didn't recognise his voice. Mum was saying no, no, I don't want to. He began to... shout, calling her things, words, I didn't understand. And then I heard him slap her. Hit her. She cried. He told her to shut up. She wouldn't, he punched her, again and again, screaming at her. I was so scared for her, it sounded like he was killing her. I hugged one of the house posts, like I wanted to merge into it. I bit it, I sang as loud as I could, anything so I wouldn't hear what was happening above me. Then the punching stopped and I heard him grunting and grunting, like a pig. There was a silence and I heard him leave and drive away. I thought she might be dead, so I kept on calling out to her. She didn't answer. I waited for a long time, it must have been hours and then I went up inside, came into here, expecting to find her dead. But she was sitting in a chair, smiling, singing to herself. I was so happy, but when I got close, I saw her face all puffed up and bruised and her lips covered in dried blood. She was putting on an act for me, pretending everything was alright and so I went along with it.

More thunder and lightning. MAE *seems stunned as if she were half expecting to hear something else. Silence.* CRESSY *is watching* NONA *closely.*

[*Moving on her as if to comfort her*] I'm sorry, Nona.

Suddenly NONA *bursts into laughter, surprising the two other sisters.*

NONA: I don't believe you.

CRESSY: Don't search for him.

NONA: [*to* CRESSY] I don't believe you. [*To* MAE] She's lying, isn't she?

An unsure MAE *shakes her head.*

CRESSY: You're right. I'm lying.

NONA: [*smiling*] You are—I can tell.

MAE: Cressy...

CRESSY: [*coldly*] What?

> *Silence.* NONA *deliberately changes the topic, by opening up the tin and smelling it.*

NONA: [*quietly*] Lost the smell of the liquorice.

END OF ACT ONE

ACT TWO

SCENE ONE

The mudflats. Night—early hours of the morning. Moonlight. NONA, *wearing her kimono and a blonde wig, enters running, yelling and screaming, carrying the Radiance tin and a stick. She runs across the stage and off, highly excited. Pause. She runs back on stage again.*

NONA: [*yelling, impatiently*] Hurry!

> *She turns and runs offstage again.*

CRESSY: [*yelling, off*] Nona!

> NONA *runs back on again.*

NONA: Hurry! [*Shouting*] See, we can walk all the way to the island.

> CRESSY *enters, her dress rolled up around her thighs. She is barefoot, wearing* NONA*'s red wig, and is carrying plastic bags.*

CRESSY: [*referring to the kimono*] Aren't you hot in that?

NONA: Fashion never sweats. [*She suddenly lunges at something in the mud and violently pokes her stick at it.*] Come out, you bugger! Shit, missed him!

CRESSY: What are you doing?

NONA: If I can't get a turtle, at least I can get a mud crab for breakfast.

CRESSY: The air's so clean and fresh.

NONA: It's better than being inside, isn't it?

CRESSY: [*dropping the bags, looking around*] Sky's cleared. Twenty-four hours ago I was in London—miserable, miserable London. [*Wriggling her toes in the mud*] Oh, I like it when the mud oozes through my toes.

NONA: You look like a bag lady. What's in them?

CRESSY: My shoes—a dress—some food—wine.

NONA: [*shouting*] Mae... hurry up! [*To* CRESSY] What a slowcoach—I bet you she doesn't want to come.

CRESSY: She said she didn't.

NONA: [*shouting*] I can see you! [*To* CRESSY] I'm going to get her!

> *Off she runs.*

CRESSY: [*gazing at the sea, to herself, almost childlike*] Water, water, everywhere and not a drop to drink… what shall we do with a drunken sailor…

NONA: [*off*] I said—come on.

> NONA *drags on a reluctant* MAE *who is wearing the wedding dress and the Doc Martens.*

Christ, you're stubborn.

MAE: This is as far as I come.

NONA: [*noticing* CRESSY *with bottle and glasses*] What's this?

CRESSY: Pit stop.

MAE: Now, you're talking.

NONA: The way we're going, we'll never get there. See, we've hardly gone any distance.

> CRESSY *takes out a half-finished bottle of wine and three glasses.*

CRESSY: [*looking back*] The house looks so small. By itself. It's a lonely house.

NONA: I bet you we didn't get all of her. [*To* MAE] We should have been out here hours ago—so much for: 'The vacuum cleaner bag is empty'. [*Tapping the Radiance tin*] I bet you half Mum's ashes is lint and dust.

MAE: Ashes to ashes, dust to dust.

> CRESSY *is giving the sisters a glass of wine each.*

CRESSY: The bottles under the sink seem to have bred, Mae.

NONA: We should get going—the tide's coming back soon and we'll never get to walk there.

MAE: It's a long walk. We need refreshments.

NONA: You don't want to go, but you will.

MAE: You can't fuckin' make me do anything.

> NONA *and* CRESSY *are surprised by* MAE*'s swearing.*

CRESSY: Look—someone's burning off their cane—it's beautiful.

MAE: Harry Wells' plantation.

NONA: Maybe he's burning it off in Mum's honour.

MAE: You're pathetically romantic.

NONA: I always think the best of people. [*Looking up at the sky*] You never see so many stars in the city.

MAE: Mum once said that those stars were our spirits. Sister stars—
for sisters. [*Pointing*] There. [*To* CRESSY] What's the name of the
constellation?

CRESSY: I forget… they were made especially for us. Girl stars.

MAE: Yes, I'd climb into your bed and we'd huddle together—

CRESSY: Looking at the sky—

MAE: Waiting for the sisters to appear. They were boring and drab when
it was day—

CRESSY: But at night they flew up into the sky—

MAE: Dressed in diamonds.

CRESSY: And all through the night they'd dance across the sky. We'd lie
there making up stories about what they did.

MAE: The princes. The parties.

CRESSY: Gossiping about the others behind our fans, keeping secrets
from them… and then dancing so fast—

MAE: We were a blur—

CRESSY: [*looking up at the sky*] Like now.

NONA: But there's only two.

MAE: You hadn't come along.

CRESSY: No, you weren't born. You've probably got your own star.

> MAE *has turned on her radio: it is dance music, possibly something
> like Dub International's version of 'Just Be Good To Me'. She starts
> to sway, humming along to the tune.* NONA *laughs affectionately.*

NONA: A bit of a rager, Mae.

MAE: Still waters run deep. [*She giggles.*] But that's what you think of
me, isn't it? Good ol' Mae. But they don't know. You don't know!

CRESSY: [*amused*] What don't they know?

MAE: [*flirtatiously*] Oh, things.

> *Faint, distant voices.*

VOICES: Come out, you old witch,
            Come out, you stupid old bitch…

CRESSY: They're out all hours. You should call the police.

NONA: I'm going to get those stones. Really give it to them this time!

MAE: Nona!

> NONA *stops. It doesn't matter.*

NONA: They might be smashing the windows or something. It's our house.

MAE: If you ignore them, they go.

NONA: No, you've got to tell people where to get off.

MAE: [*still swaying to the music*] They're only throwing stones on the roof. It doesn't matter. They'll go. They'll soon get bored. God created teenage boys to make one doubt that intelligent life exists on earth.

NONA: A teenage boy is going to make my fortune.

CRESSY: What do you mean?

NONA: Shorty. [*Yelling at the boys, brandishing her stick*] I'm gonna come and break every bone in your bodies!

CRESSY: Who's Shorty?

NONA: A snooker player. One night I was playing pool and I see this boy and I think to myself: he's brilliant. A bit moody, like all artists, but a genius. I'm going to be his manager.

CRESSY: I thought you were going to run a wig shop?

NONA: I'm not keen on that idea now.

MAE: He's a boy?

NONA: Almost. He's sixteen.

MAE: You're managing a sixteen-year-old snooker player?

NONA: He's won the Victorian championship and he'll win the world championship by the time he's eighteen. We'll go to England next month, hustle a bit of money.

MAE: Do you… I mean, do you—

NONA: He'd like to. But I said only when he wins the world championship. He'll be eighteen then. I'm no cradle snatcher. [*Pause.*] Why you both looking at me like that? It's a job. I could make a packet. I really believe in Shorty. He calls me 'Boss', that's great, isn't it—to be called Boss?

The boys have stopped singing.

MAE: See, they've gone. I hate this song.

In the process of turning off the radio, it falls in the mud.

NONA: You're going to ruin it.

MAE: Doesn't matter.

NONA: Why? You stole that too? You could end up in jail again.

MAE: I was never in jail. Is that what you've been telling people? I was never in jail.

NONA: I read it in the paper.

MAE: Good behaviour.

CRESSY: For what?

MAE: I fell in love. [*Pause.*] I was a charge nurse, he was a surgeon.

NONA: Married, of course.

MAE *gives her a quizzical look of 'How do you know?'*

All doctors are married, Mae—even the gay ones.

MAE: His wife was very attractive.

NONA: Kids?

MAE: Of course, why do things in half measures? [*To* CRESSY] So bad did I want him that I showered him with presents. A watch at first. A briefcase. I couldn't stop. I swamped the poor man with presents. Beautiful things. There's a word for someone who has a compulsion to steal, right? There must be a word for someone who is a compulsive gift-giver. He couldn't believe it. Where did I get the money from, he asked. I have an inheritance, I said. He even got his wife to ring me and tell me to stop sending him presents.

CRESSY: His wife?

MAE: Yeah, she was pretty matter of fact about it. [*Bursting into laughter*] An inheritance! All the time I was nicking the money from the nurses' fund. They eventually noticed—it was quite a sum, even if I do say so myself—and called in the police. I was the last suspect. Charge nurse Sister McKenna—duty bound, morally upright: there was no way I would be responsible.

CRESSY: Did you go to jail?

MAE: Did I do time? No. Good behaviour bond and I had to pay back the money. [*Beat.*] I did my time here—with Mum.

CRESSY: You had nowhere else to go.

MAE: I was ashamed. Not because I stole the money, but because he gave evidence for me. So did his wife. So condescending on the witness stand—'She's a bit sad, I don't hate her.' I must have seemed a right idiot. [*Pause.*] Still waters run deep, Nona. Beneath this perfect exterior beats the heart of a criminal.

NONA: [*to* CRESSY] See, I told you she was a criminal.

MAE: Not half the criminal your father was.

NONA *is irritated by* MAE*'s condescension, but tries not to show it by laughing out loud.*

NONA: I'm still going to go searching for him.

CRESSY: Nona…

NONA: If I saw him, I would have to love him, because he's me. I am part of his flesh and blood like Mum was. I'd forgive him. Is that terrible?

CRESSY: No.

NONA: [*looking to* MAE] You wouldn't?

MAE: I couldn't, Nono. Not a man who raped her. Raped any woman.

> NONA *grabs* MAE*'s arm.*

NONA: This flesh and blood is half his.

MAE: This flesh and blood is also his father's and his father's father, just as Mum's blood is her mother's mother's. The blood stretches back until the first man and woman. He's not half your blood.

NONA: Hey, I never thought of it that way. Then it makes sense to forgive him. He'd have their blood. He may be a rotten sod, but his father could have been quite a nice bloke and his mother fantastic.

MAE: You're incorrigible.

NONA: I don't want to think bad about anyone.

MAE: Maybe you should. It's called a sense of morality.

NONA: Morality is made up by people so they can tell other people what to do.

MAE: Some people need that.

NONA: You should talk—you stole things.

MAE: I'm not talking—

NONA: You're so uptight. What you need is a good… enema. Didn't you notice when you were a nurse how much happier people looked after they had one? That's what everyone should have. People should be happy. Think positive thoughts. Mum wasn't perfect. I think of her good points. Life is not dirt. My father was not perfect. No man is.

MAE: Sometimes you have to make a decision and say that something is evil or else you'll forgive evil acts.

NONA: I can't think that anyone is evil, that anyone is dirt.

MAE: Some people are—Harry Wells is. He's dirt. I'll get him! [*Calling out*] I'll get you!

> *Pause.*

NONA: If you're going to be like that… We don't have to talk on our walk—some music then.

NONA *goes to the radio to search for some music.* MAE *walks towards the house, stops and stares at it.*

MAE: [*to herself*] I don't have the courage.

CRESSY: What?

MAE: Nothing.

CRESSY *notices* MAE *rubbing her face as if it is tight and tired.*

CRESSY: Put your face in a bowl of cracked ice for half an hour every morning.

MAE: You're joking?

CRESSY: No.

MAE: Do you want me to hold my breath too?

CRESSY: It helps the skin.

The radio station is the religious one.

DOYLE: [*voiceover*] 'Our Church is only halfway in its restoration fund. Mr and Mrs Furbank yesterday contributed two hundred and fifty dollars, for which we are eternally grateful…'

NONA: [*laughing*] Hey, the one I gave a hard-on to!

CRESSY: I do it.

MAE: [*becoming agitated, quietly*] Turn it off, Nono.

NONA: No, he's funny.

DOYLE: 'You see, it is little deeds that will add up to one great deed. The Catholic Women's Auxiliary will be holding a stall in the main street on Saturday. There will be second-hand books, cakes, and knick-knacks. I would also like to send a cheerio to Mrs Hamilton who is in the Girrawandi Base Hospital, with what we all hope is just a temporary setback. Also in hospital is one of our staunchest churchgoers, Tom Davies, who is on the way to a complete recovery after his tractor accident. All the best, Tom.'

CRESSY: It just refreshes the skin.

MAE: Why don't I just put my face in the freezer, no-one can see it then.

CRESSY: Come on, Mae.

NONA *is laughing at the priest.*

MAE: [*to* CRESSY] Does it help you forget who you are?

CRESSY: Mae, what has got into you—

MAE: I said, 'Turn it off'.

She rushes over, pushes NONA *away and turns it off.*

NONA: Hey!

MAE: Listen to me. I said, 'Turn it off. Turn it off'.

MAE *starts to feverishly bury the radio in the mud.*

NONA: Hey, what are you doing?

MAE: The hypocritical bastard… I poured out my heart to him and he was so condescending.

She laughs as the priest's voice disappears.

Anyway, I'm giving him a burial. More than he gave Mum.

NONA: Hey, I wanted to listen to that.

MAE: I can do anything I like. You know why? Because I earned it. [*To* NONA] And you earned nothing. [*Sarcastically to* CRESSY] Put your face in a bowl of ice! [*To both*] Put your heads in the sand.

NONA: All because I turned on the radio.

MAE: Shut up! [*Pointing to the Radiance tin*] I sat and watched you! I came up here. She was ill, but she was disappointed it wasn't you, or you. She lived like a derelict. I told her lies. [*To* CRESSY] You were overseas, you'd be home soon. [*To* NONA] You had an important job down south. [*Yelling*] You understand! You understand how every time I told those lies why you weren't here, I hated you. I hated your selfishness. I hated you!

CRESSY: I know how you feel.

MAE: You don't know. Who are you? Who is me? [*Thumping her chest*] Who is me? I'd ask her again and again. But she wouldn't. [*Pointing to the tin*] That thing wouldn't, wouldn't tell me. She'd sooner keep it a secret, rather than tell her daughter. And yet, I looked after her. I cleaned and washed her—

CRESSY: [*angrily*] Because you had nowhere to go. You were hiding here.

MAE: I came here because I was afraid. And humiliated. To go to court, to be called a criminal… do you know how humiliating that is? I came here because I wanted to know. I wanted to know where I came from, how I ended up the way I did. I wanted to know about my father. My relatives. I'd take her down to the beach and I'd point to the island. I'd ask her: What happened, how did my great-great-grandparents get thrown off the island? She wouldn't answer. [*Beat.*] Sometimes she and I would talk. Not much. Sometimes she even said thank you when I bathed her. [*To* CRESSY] I couldn't leave her. Too much of a sense of duty. Same old Mae. Isn't she a trouper? Isn't she just the best?

NONA: Look, I'm grateful for what you did.

MAE: Are you? Aren't you more interested in a sixteen-year-old snooker player?

NONA: Christ Almighty.

MAE: I'll tell you. I'll tell you the reason I didn't run away, the reason why I didn't hide like you two—

NONA: Stop being the martyr—

MAE: I'm just telling you what happened. I want you to hear.

NONA: What would you know?

MAE: I know you don't want to, because you like to avoid anything remotely resembling responsibility. Because I don't know you, I know you.

NONA: What does that mean?

MAE: The first time… the first time I knew something was really wrong… she came into my room with something in her hands. She was really puzzled: 'This fell out of my body, what is it?' She had a handful of shit. I took her to the doctor. Premature senility. I hadn't noticed until then, I just thought she was going eccentric in her old age. She got worse and worse. Sometimes she'd just mumble to herself. Other times sing. Those were the best times. Other times she'd yell and yell at me, scream at me. Hour after hour, until she went hoarse. I had no idea why, except, in her deepest of hearts, she hated me.

CRESSY: She didn't hate you—

MAE: Let me finish. Listen to me. [*Yelling*] Listen to me! Listen to your sister! In church she would be quiet. Something about the ceremony that calmed her. One morning she was receiving communion and you know what she did? [*Laughing*] She bit Father Doyle's finger, nearly clean off. So no communion. In biting that finger, something in our glorious mother finally snapped. I couldn't even take her to church because she began to yell out things, obscene things, demented things, until we weren't allowed to go anymore. When I tried to clean her, she bit me, screamed at me, until I had to give up. One day I was passing that rundown hall near Johnson's Crossing. I heard people inside singing hymns. They sounded happy, so I thought I'd take her there. It was a revivalist church. When we were inside she was quiet because she recognised the look in their eyes, they had a fire like she did. They all believed in the Apocalypse. An old farmer got up and started to speak in tongues and Mum leapt up and she spoke in tongues and they let her, thinking she was possessed by God. Eventually even they understood she was possessed by madness, not by God. The next Sunday—see, she no longer understood what day of the week it was—but she instinctively understood like some dog might, that it was the time of the week to go for a walk. I had to fight her from going. She slapped me away and headed off down the road, screaming in tongues, at some children who were half scared, half amused by her. I dragged her back down the road. The children followed us laughing and yelling out, 'Witch, witch'. She bit me and tried to run away. I caught her and dragged her back into the house. I tied her, like an animal, to her chair. She ate at the ropes until her gums bled, until she was so exhausted she gave in. That's what I had to do at the end. Every night I tied her to her bed and then after untying her in the morning I'd tie her into her chair. She screamed at me in tongues, until I thought I was going mad, and I'd put my hands around her throat. One time I squeezed that throat so hard that she went purple—I only stopped from killing her when I saw the fear in her eyes and that fear made her human again instead of the monster I was living with. Then, on the morning of the last day, she stopped screaming at me and was looking at me, speaking in tongues, but looking at me: with love? I didn't know. I pleaded with her: tell me, tell me once in your life that you love me. Tell me, Mum. Tell me that you love me. [*She sinks to her knees.*] And then, like she was possessed by the devil, she found this energy and she started to scream at me, her eyes on fire. Scream and scream!

NONA *moves away, frightened.*

NONA: [*to* CRESSY] Get her to stop!

But CRESSY *doesn't know what to do, she is mesmerised by* MAE*'s pain.*

MAE: And I screamed back.

She demonstrates, screaming in tongues, now fully caught up in it as if NONA *and* CRESSY *aren't there.*

And in this language I was saying, 'I hate you, I hate you, I want to kill you!' [*A moment of lucidity*] I wasn't out when she died. See, I was there, she was there, tied up and we were screaming at each other. [*She begins to cry.*] All I wanted was for her to tell me once, just once: 'I love you, Mae.'

> MAE *is screaming out in tongues again.* CRESSY *kneels down and hugs her.*

CRESSY: Mae!

> MAE *suddenly stops.*

MAE: Who is she? Who is that Mae? [*Softly*] I've got nothing. Nothing.

CRESSY: Shhhh, you have. Us. The house.

MAE: I haven't got the house.

NONA: [*still apprehensive*] Yes, we have. It's ours.

MAE: It's not.

CRESSY: It belonged to Mum.

MAE: It was always Harry's. You know why that fucker's burning off his cane now—because he can't sleep. That woman, Mum, was walking down the main street with me and saw Harry and she spat on him. In the middle of the street. In front of everyone. She yelled stuff at him and the whole town knew he knew her. Knew her? He fucked her and Mum thought it was love. His lawyer sent me a note this morning saying Harry was taking the house back.

NONA: It's not ours?

MAE: No.

NONA: When do we have to leave?

MAE: 'Twenty-four hours to vacate the premises.' Tomorrow morning.

NONA: There'll be no money, then?

MAE: No money. [*A beat. To* NONA] He's dirt.

> NONA *is stunned by these turn of events.*

NONA: [*half to herself*] Nothing...

CRESSY: Why didn't you tell me?

MAE: Because I didn't want you to feel sorry for me. You're always sorry for me. And I wanted to do it by myself.

CRESSY: Do what?

> *Pause.*

MAE: Burn down the house.

CRESSY: [*astonished*] The house?

MAE: Burn it right down. I didn't think you two would be here. I thought I'd set fire to it. And Harry'd get there too late. He'd see flames in the distance, think it was someone firing their cane and then—'Fuck a duck!—It's my house!' He arrives and it's only embers.

NONA: You weren't serious.

MAE: Absolutely. Get my own back on this town. Get my revenge on Harry—Mum's revenge. [*Beat.*] I had it all planned. Tonight. Sitting out here watching it.

   Silence.

CRESSY: Do it.

NONA: What?

CRESSY: Do it now. Burn it down. I'll help.

NONA: You two are crazy.

CRESSY: Do you want to?

MAE: No, it was a stupid idea. Like stealing that money.

CRESSY: Do it! Look at it, Mae, it's just a shack.

MAE: No, I think I went crazy—it's just a crazy—

NONA: You're fucking right there—

CRESSY: You're stupid now, Mae. Burn it, that's the logical thing.

MAE: Cressy! Don't!

CRESSY: Burn it. We'll help you!

NONA: I bloody won't.

CRESSY: You'll regret it, Mae. You'll look back and think I should have burnt it—got rid of it!

NONA: Two wacko sisters—listen to yourselves.

CRESSY: It'll make everything easy after that. It'll be gone. That fucking house will be gone.

   NONA *is astonished at* CRESSY*'s swearing.*

NONA: What's got into you?

CRESSY: I'll help you. We'll burn it to the ground. You won't have to do it by yourself. I'll help you. Do you want to?

NONA: Don't!

CRESSY: Mae— [*Pause.*] Do you want to?

   Pause.

MAE: Christ, yeah—
NONA: No—
MAE: I've got all this kerosene under the house.

> CRESSY *laughs.*

Be prepared.
CRESSY: Then let's do it.
NONA: My clothes!
MAE: We'll put our stuff into my car.
NONA: You can't burn it. They'll jail us!
CRESSY: [*to* MAE] Come on.
MAE: [*to* NONA] Give me the tin.
NONA: [*stepping away*] Why?
MAE: I'll put Mum in there—the house will be her grave.
NONA: [*hugging tin*] No bloody way. We scatter her properly. You can't burn her twice.
CRESSY: [*excited*] I want to see it burn. Let's do it.
MAE: Fantastic!

> *They run off like kids, laughing.*

NONA: [*shouting after them*] They'll know we've done it!

> *She hurries after them.*

SCENE TWO

The mudflats. An hour later. A distant glow from where the house is on fire. MAE *runs on excited.*

MAE: It's really burning! It's really happening!

> *She is squealing with delight, jumping up and down, looking back at the burning house.* NONA *comes on, nervous and worried.*

NONA: Holy hell. It's going. What have we done? We're going to be jailed for this. The cops are gonna get us. Stupid Cressy…

> *She puts the Radiance tin to one side and squats.*

MAE: What are you doing?
NONA: Whenever I'm nervous, I've really got to piss. The cops will get us for sure.

MAE: [*to* NONA] We'll blame the boys who throw stones on the roof.

NONA: You've really got a criminal mind, Mae.

> CRESSY *enters, part of one hand burnt, though she doesn't seem to notice it, her dress torn, and part of the hem still smouldering. She gazes, as if mesmerised by the fire.*

You're still burning!

> CRESSY *absent-mindedly pats out the smouldering hem, all the time watching the fire.*

You were lucky, you know. The house up in flames and you under the house looking for more kerosene! Great!

> CRESSY *picks up the Radiance tin.*

Hey!

CRESSY: [*watching the fire with the tin, quietly*] Come on, Mum, watch it go... it's just memories now.

MAE: [*shouting*] Can you see it, Harry?! That's your house, Harry! Can you see it? It's going to be ashes, Harry. Burn, baby, burn! [*She is dancing in the mud now. To* CRESSY] Isn't this the best bonfire you've ever seen?

CRESSY: [*quietly, lost in thought*] Yes. Yes it is.

NONA: [*noticing*] You've burnt your hand.

CRESSY: [*gazing at it as if it belongs to someone else*] It's only flesh.

> MAE *starts gently singing 'I'll Tell My Ma'.*

MAE: I'll tell my ma when I go home,
> The boys won't leave the girls alone...

> MAE *looks at* NONA *who returns a nervous smile.*

NONA: [*singing, again gently, slowly*]
> They pulled my hair, they stole my comb,
> Well, that's alright till I get home.

CRESSY: [*singing the chorus but almost timidly*]
> She is handsome, she is pretty,
> She is the belle of Dublin City—

> *She stops.*

It should be—

MAE: Belfast City—

NONA: [*to* CRESSY] But your father came from Dublin.
CRESSY: I don't know. [*To the tin*] Only you know.

    Pause.

MAE: [*to* NONA] She taught you that song.
NONA: When she was happy, she'd launch into it.
CRESSY: No, softly at first.

    Demonstrating:

        I'll tell my ma when I go home,
        The boys won't leave the girls alone.

    CRESSY *begins to sway as her mother did. The other two join in, singing slowly and swaying.*

ALL: [*singing*]

        They pulled my hair, they stole my comb,
        Well that's alright till I get home.

    The pace gets faster as they go into the chorus.

        She is handsome, she is pretty,
        She is the belle of Dublin city,
        She is courting one, two, three,
        Please, won't you tell me who is she?

    NONA *starts, but the others soon join her, dancing on the mudflats, linking arm in arm and then clapping as they perform a joyous, loud version of the song.*

        Albert Mooney says he loves her,
        All the boys are fighting for her,
        They knock at the door and ring at the bell,
        Saying, 'Oh, my true love, are you well?'
        Let the wind and rain and hail blow high,
        And the snow come tumbling from the sky,
        She's as nice as apple pie,
        She'll get her own lad by and by.
        When she gets a lad of her own,
        She won't tell her ma when she gets home.
        Let them all come as they will,
        For it's Albert Mooney she loves still.

Towards the end of the song they have been dancing wildly, almost possessed, their energy reminding us of how they must have been at their happiest when they were girls, getting rid of the tension of the night. They stop, panting, perspiring, but happy.

CRESSY: The only thing—

MAE: [*laughing*] The only thing she taught us all.

CRESSY: 'I'll Tell My Ma'.

They laugh. Silence. They look at one another. The song has brought them together.

MAE: The mud's shining. Like it's on fire.

NONA: We'll walk across hot coals to get there. A strong wind.

MAE: It won't last long.

NONA: I've been wondering. Once we get there, where do we scatter her ashes?

CRESSY: She may not have wanted that, Nona.

NONA: She loved to listen to the sea. [*Beat.*] We're scattered, like Mum, like her mum. [*Beaming*] But we'll take her home. [*Beat.*] And we'll have to do that for each other.

CRESSY: Nona—it's too late. We'll bury her in the cemetery. Let's just watch the house burn.

NONA: I want to go. Why don't you want to? The sun's coming up. Come on, we'll have to hurry to get to the island before the tide comes in.

CRESSY: No—you go. Run. Go on—

NONA: Come with me.

CRESSY *shakes her head.*

Mae—

MAE: It's too late—tomorrow. We'll take the ferry.

NONA: It's today. Today!

CRESSY: Scatter them here—on the mudflats. Then let the tide take them where it wants to.

NONA: No—back to where her grandparents came from. First the whites, now the Japs. Let's take her back. Come on, you came especially for her funeral—well, then—let's make it special—

CRESSY: I didn't come for her—I knew you'd be here.

NONA: She's our mother—

CRESSY: I came here to see you. [*Pause.*] Go on—if you run you'll make it.

NONA: Looks like just me, then.

MAE: It's only ashes.

NONA: [*teasing, taunting*] I'll stay there and get the ferry back. Maybe the Black Prince is on the island. I've always dreamed I'd meet him somewhere. Wouldn't recognise him. Just this cute older man. I'd go to bed with him—

CRESSY: Nona!

NONA: We'd be hot, sweaty—I'd be really wet, not only between the legs but all over. And we'd be sliding all over the place. [*She picks up the Radiance tin.*] Big chest—this big dick inside me—

CRESSY: Shut the hell up.

NONA: And I wouldn't know it was my father until the morning. He'd be really huge—the best lover I've ever had… I'd be having this orgasm, the best I've ever had, with this big dick—bursting inside me—coming inside me—his daughter—and he'd be watching me moaning, moaning—

CRESSY: [*screaming*] Shut up!

She rushes at NONA, *throws her to the ground, and pushes her face into the mud.*

Shut up! Shut your dirty filthy mouth. Eat it. That's what you think— eat it.

MAE: [*trying to pull* CRESSY *off*] Stop it—stop—

CRESSY: Shut her up, shut her dirty mouth—dirty mind—

NONA: You're fucked. Get away from me.

CRESSY *is angry and anguished.*

CRESSY: You were created from dirt—your father was dirt! He never raped her. [*Beat.*] It was me. He raped me!

NONA *gives an astonished laugh.*

Under the house.

Pause.

NONA: Bullshit.

CRESSY: Me! He did it to me! [*Pause.*] Under that burning house. [*To* MAE] Me. Me playing under the house. He grunting like a pig. Hands under my dress, stabbing me in two. And I am moaning, moaning in pain, Nona. [*Pause.*] He was just one of Mum's boyfriends. If he walked down the street I don't think I'd even recognise him. He was going to drive away but his car had no petrol, so he went and bought a can. Mum laughed at him coughing and spluttering as he sucked on a tube to get it flowing into the tank. Then she went into town. I was playing under the house, and had forgotten him entirely when suddenly he was there putting his hands up my dress. I said no, but he hit me across the face. I struggled and screamed but he was too strong. He forced me up against one of the house posts. As he was doing it he kept kissing me with his mouth smelling of petrol. The pain. All this awful pain through my body like he was stabbing me in two. It was so excruciating that I bit into the post, wanting to bite it in two. He grunting like a pig, biting me in the shoulder, his saliva in my ear. When he finished he warned me not to tell Mum but I wasn't quick enough in answering him, so he shoved the handle of a screwdriver up my rectum—I was crying out in agony—and he warned me that if I told anyone, anyone, about what had happened he would come back and put the screwdriver right through me. Then he drove away. I stayed under the house for hours crying and crying, trying to clean myself with some old rags. I didn't tell Mum. Then a few months later I realised I was having that man's baby. I tried to keep it from her until it was too late. You know what happened when I told her—she hit me. She said I was lying. That it wasn't her boyfriend—that it was one of the local boys and I was blaming him. She didn't believe me.

NONA: You're lying again.

CRESSY: I had you in that house. In my bed. Only Mum knew. I was twelve. Twelve, Nona… [*Pause.*] I hated Mum for not believing me. But at least she kept you, pretended you were hers. [*Motioning to the tin*] That's not your mother. I'm your mother, Nona.

NONA: [*waving the stick at her*] Stay away from me.

CRESSY: You were born because your so-called Black Prince raped me.

NONA: I don't believe you.

CRESSY: Just a filthy pig smelling of petrol.

NONA: You want to hurt me.

CRESSY: [*to* MAE] Mum and I kept it a secret. I was ashamed. She was ashamed.

NONA: That's not true.

CRESSY: But I'm not ashamed of you. I'm telling you the truth. You're my flesh, my daughter.

NONA: Liar!

CRESSY: You're my blood. My blood is yours, Nona! Once I heard Mum was dead, I came back for you. I named you, because you were mine. That's all Mum would allow me to do—name you. Nona.

NONA: [backing away, using her stick to keep CRESSY at bay] No. [Referring to the ashes] This tin is my mother. You're my sister.

CRESSY: I came back to see you. I want you to know the truth. You have to learn the truth. No more secrets and lies, Nona.

NONA: No. I'm going to scatter my mother's ashes. You're a liar.

CRESSY: Don't go. The tide's coming in.

NONA: I don't care! I'm going to scatter my mother's ashes. Then I'm going to find the Black Prince. I was not born from dirt.

NONA *runs off, crossing the mudflats.*

CRESSY: Nona! [She slips and falls in the mud.] Nona!

NONA: [off, crying out] I was not born from dirt!

MAE *goes to* CRESSY.

CRESSY: [crying out] Nona! [She goes to run after her, but slips again in the mud. Worried] The tide's coming in.

MAE: She'll make it… she'll make it. [Pause.] You kept it so long. Near the end when she was dotty she said some things and I put two and two together.

CRESSY: [looking at the distant burning house] It's good to see it go. To burn it all away. Nona's my child.

MAE *is sitting in the mud with* CRESSY. MAE *puts her head in* CRESSY*'s lap and* CRESSY *strokes her hair.*

MAE: Eventually—she'll come around.

CRESSY: I want to love her.

MAE: She's a born survivor. All us three are.

CRESSY: [bemused] Sort of.

MAE: The sun's coming up. Our stars are disappearing.

CRESSY: The sisters are going. [Pause.] Look how fast she's running.

Pause.

MAE: [*looking at the house*] Just embers now.
CRESSY: [*smiling*] Yes. Gone.

> *She sings softly as she strokes* MAE*'s hair.*

> She is handsome, she is pretty,
> She is the belle of Dublin city,
> She is courting one, two, three,
> Please, won't you tell me, who is she?

> *Shallow water begins to lap around them, but they don't notice;
> they're watching the house burn down to the ground.*

THE END

ALSO BY LOUIS NOWRA AND AVAILABLE FROM CURRENCY PRESS

The Boyce Trilogy
A story of a dynasty, and the money, love and madness that lie within.

Cosi
The classic Australian epic about theatre, madness, illusion, sanity and life.

The Golden Age
Haunting play about a group discovered in the wilds of Tasmania in 1939. Lost in time and steeped in its own history and traditions, the community is a disturbing challenge to its modern counterpart.

Inner Voices and Albert Names Edward
Two of Nowra's earliest plays, these vividly demonstrate his early preoccupation with isolation and the exercise of power through the imagination.

The Language of the Gods
Set in Sulawesi in 1946, this play is a powerful human drama about people whose lives are set to change forever.

Summer of the Aliens
Semi-autobiographical, this play presents a moving and amusing evocation of a family and neighbourhood in Melbourne, 1962.

Visions
Set during the War of the Triple Alliance, the bloodiest conflict in Latin American history, when visions of the arts of peace sacrifice a nation to its own barbarity.